King Donkey Ears

Retold by Lesley Sims

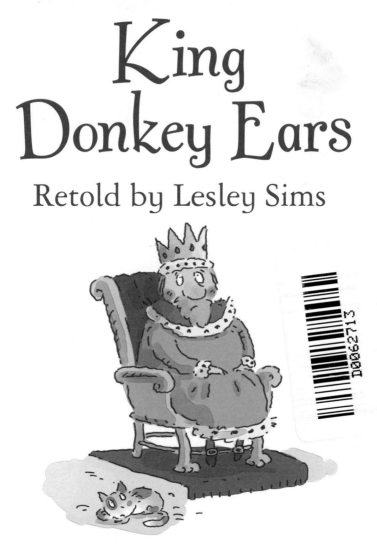

Illustrated by
Mike and Carl Gordon

Reading consultant: Alison Kelly
Roehampton University

This story is
about a king,

Meg,
a servant,

the king's
best friend,

a tree,

a woodcutter

and a harp.

There was once a king
with a big secret.

He didn't even tell his
best friend.

No one knew...
except the servant
who cut his hair.

Every month, the king had a hair cut.

Snip!

Then he sent the servant to prison.

In July, it was Meg's turn.

Meg saw the king's ears.

She was shocked, but
she didn't say.

9

As soon as Meg had finished, the king cried,

Off to jail!

"But my mother is sick," said Meg. "She needs me."

The king thought of his own mother.

He didn't like putting people in jail.

"Okay," said the king. "Promise you'll never tell anyone."

I promise!

That night, it was all
Meg could think about.

She had to tell.

At last, she had an idea.
She wouldn't tell anyone.

She'd tell a tree!

So she did. Now Meg
felt much better.

Later, a woodcutter
chopped down the tree.

The tree became a harp.

One day, the king gave
a huge concert.

But the new harp played
a very strange tune.

"You told my secret!"
the king roared at Meg.

The king's best friend
came forward.

"It's not a secret," he
said. "We all know."

"And you don't mind?"
asked the king.

"Of course not!"

23

So the king freed all
the servants.

24

And he learned to love
his ears.

PUZZLES

Puzzle 1

Put the pictures in order.

A

B

C

D

E

Puzzle 2

Can you spot the differences
between these two pictures?
There are six to find.

Puzzle 3
Find these things in the
picture:

cat   chair   crown

flower   king   Meg

Answers to puzzles

Puzzle 1

C   D   B   E   A

Puzzle 2

Puzzle 3

About King Donkey Ears

King Donkey Ears is based on an Irish folk tale, but that came from a much older legend about a king named Midas.

King Midas was asked to judge a competition between a musician and the god Apollo. King Midas declared the musician the winner – and even said he was the better player. Apollo was so angry, he gave King Midas donkey's ears.

Designed by Caroline Spatz
Series designer: Russell Punter

First published in 2009 by Usborne Publishing Ltd., Usborne House,
83-85 Saffron Hill, London EC1N 8RT, England. www.usborne.com
Copyright © 2009 Usborne Publishing Ltd.